5 Acts of Courage:

FROM CRISIS TO THRIVING

5 Life-Affirming Strategies to Help Families Recover and
Heal from the Trauma of Loved Ones Suffering from the
Disease of Addiction

KL WELLS

5 Acts of Courage: From Crisis to Thriving

5 Life-Affirming Strategies to Help Families Recover and Heal
from the Trauma of Loved Ones
Suffering from the Disease of Addiction

©2023 KL Wells
kl@voicesincourage.com
voicesincourage.com

ISBN: 978-0-98941951-2

"From Crisis to Thriving" content created by the
National Fallen Firefighters Foundation

• • •

Author's Note

The experiences I write about in this book are uniquely mine, although they will be familiar to those who love someone suffering from Substance Abuse Disorder. The information and resources provided in this book are among the many tools I used successfully to navigate through one of the most challenging times in my life-tools and resources that I still make use of today. I offer both my experiences and the information presented in this book to help and inspire anyone seeking a healthier, more positive way to be with an addicted loved one. Each of us is different and the challenges we face walking this path are diverse. Positive changes and the timing of those changes will, of course, vary for each individual. I believe we can each heal from the trauma and chaos we experience with an addicted loved one. I also believe that the help offered in this book, taken even in the smallest measure, can create a point of light to follow that can lead us out of crisis and into living our best life.

• • •

Book & Cover Design
Madison Wooters/Madison Wooters Design
mnwcreativedesign.com

Publications Management
Eva Long/Long On Books
longonbooks.com

Printed in USA

• • •

To Sam

*Without you unknowingly stepping into this courageous journey,
none of what has followed would have been possible.
As dark as that journey has been for you,
I always saw your light shining through,
guiding you to transcend this disease and thrive.*

To Patty

*There is no better person for me
to have gone through Sam's crisis with.
You challenged me and supported me,
always having my best interests at heart.
Your love is the foundation upon which I stand.*

To Diane Lachel

*My dearest friend and spiritual teacher, you joined my journey
wholeheartedly, travelling with me from
crisis to thriving without judgment,
bringing your joy and wisdom to the adventure ahead.*

To Callie & Kevin Crumpacker, Kanaychowa Layman & Sparkle

*As my powerful tribe, you held me with such love,
compassion and possibilities during my Vision Quest and beyond.
You walked with me every step of the way.
You are why I do this work.*

• • •

5 Acts of Courage

Introduction

Dear families and loves ones of addicts and alcoholics,

Sometimes life just falls apart in order for it all to genuinely fall together. This is true for what happened to me and it's true for countless more families who find themselves searching for answers in the midst of the utter despair, insanity, chaos, and heartbreak we feel when someone we love has an addiction. Some lives have fallen apart and are only surviving day to day with a loved one's life-threatening illness. There are others who are struggling to put devastated parts of their lives back together to find some normalcy despite endless chaos.

Like the phoenix, the legendary bird in ancient Greek mythology, I believe we can achieve new life by rising from the ashes of an old one, especially out of crisis when we must decide who we will choose to be in order to meet a seemingly overwhelming challenge. I believe we can all rise above being just an expert at surviving each crisis that is inevitably part of our loved one's disease. I believe we can rise to live our best life, not only for our own peace and well being, but to serve as an authentic contribution to our addicted loved one.

On a sunny Tuesday morning, August 28, 2018, I arrived for a scheduled meeting in my role as executive coach for a multimillion-dollar company whose executive team I had been working with for several years. As I made my way to the conference room, I felt something not right—a profound heaviness among a normally energetic staff. In the conference room, those sitting around the table looked like they were in shock. The CEO was absent. I was then told that over the weekend the CEO's son had died of a drug overdose.

So I did what I have extensive experience doing: I immediately stepped into that storm of grief and chaos and became a presence of calm among confusion and trauma. My own focus in that meeting shifted to hold the space for them, steadfast and resolute, and help them navigate through this traumatic event.

What this executive team could not have known then, nor would it have been appropriate to tell them at that time, was that on the very night the CEO's son passed away, I had witnessed my 27-year-old son's arrest for a crime committed while in a drug-induced psychosis and extreme paranoia.

On that weekend, from my fourth-story hotel window in Puyallup, Washington, where my wife, Patty, and I had traveled that weekend to visit Sam, I had watched him below, walking up a hill towards our hotel, then saw with horror police cars pulling up right behind him, doors open, guns drawn, yelling "Drop to your knees!" I raced down the hotel stairwell and what followed is forever etched in my mind: Surrounded by police, I watched in shock and disbelief as my son, on his knees, was handcuffed at gunpoint.

In that moment, every dream I ever held for him shattered on that sidewalk along with everything I believed about my own ability to help him beat his addiction. Our lives now and forever changed, my heart deeply wounded. My son, having been a responsible homeowner, earning an excellent salary as the most highly credentialed employee for his age in his chosen profession, soon-to-be engaged and enthusiastically embraced by his girlfriend's family, had hit bottom with his addiction—bottom, at least in my view. What lay ahead for him was as yet unknown to both of us.

By now Patty had joined me and we both watched Sam's arrest. I was certain I was living the worst moment of my life, but I was wrong when I saw my son's stricken face. Sam's eyes locked onto mine, and he called out, "Mom! Mom!" the entire time, in full desperation, pleading with me to save him as four police officers wrestled him into the police car. Helpless to do anything for him or to influence the situation in any other way—that moment nearly destroyed me.

How familiar is a story like this? How many people do we know who have been through a version of this? How many of us believe our lives have become only about surviving our loved ones' addiction day to day, feeling desperate to change what's happening, the heart-wrenching pain, the mind-numbing shock? How many of us have been overwhelmed by disbelief, denial, shame, guilt, pain, anger, depression, hopelessness, and resignation—felt all at once in an emotional torrent or in stages, draining us in bits and pieces?

How many of us find our lives hijacked by a disease we are ill-prepared to deal with?

On that sidewalk, police cars finally moving away, my son in the back seat of one of them, I somehow held myself together emotionally until the cars were out of sight. Patty and I walked back to our hotel room. Once inside, I sank to my knees, sobbing uncontrollably.

After a while, spent, I got to my feet, wiped my tears, and made a commitment to find a way to live through what had just happened, not by staggering through life with a brave face to the world, keeping my pain and anguish a secret, but choosing instead to dig deep into the core of my being, through my own depths of despair and anguish and commit to stepping up to something greater for myself that would contribute to Sam as well.

This event with Sam brought me to my breaking point, no question, yet I've been no stranger to the depths of pain and depression one can travel living with and/or loving an addict. I am the daughter of a prescription drug abuser, the sister of a cocaine addict, the former spouse of an alcoholic suffering from

PTSD. I'm the mother of a son who has been both addicted and sober since he was 13. I am now married to a 30-year recovering alcoholic, and I am a friend to a multitude of friends who are each grappling with addicted loved ones.

Having lived through three generations of addiction in my family, it seems I have been training my entire life to gain the skills to experience my feelings, take care of myself, build a community of people who can provide steady support, to explore my own beliefs, and learn everything I could about this disease and what we can do besides feeling frozen with helplessness or engaging in sure-to-fail efforts to control outcomes.

Every cycle of crises with my family has challenged me to dig deeper within myself, to increase my spirit, strength, compassion, and love over the course of my life—to elevate my game on this journey we call Life, to use everything Life brought to me to learn and grow. But now Sam's arrest and the condition he was in had increased his risks exponentially and raised me to a whole new level of personal work as well.

I knew there were lessons to be learned here and I was going to lean into embracing the opportunity to learn them. But first, I needed to feel, to sleep, and to recover.

On the drive home from Washington, when I had finally collected myself, I knew the next right step for me in that moment was to call my best friend, Diane, the one person I knew who could hear me without judgment, respond with compassion, and advise me on the people I needed to talk to next.

If someone had told me that from broken dreams on a sidewalk I would embark on a journey of exploration and learning that would lead me to help other families learn an entirely new way of approaching this disease, I wouldn't have, couldn't have, imagined it. Yet, through my own journey, a community of courageous voices and trailblazing resources have been created that can help everyone rediscover themselves and strengthen their resilience to move through frustration and powerlessness and see more positive possibilities for themselves as they struggle to solve this problem of their addicted loved ones.

Voices InCourage —
A Game-Changing Approach to Loving Those Dealing with Substance Abuse Disorder

Welcome to Voices InCourage.

As mothers, fathers, spouses, sisters, brothers, grandparents, friends, aunts and uncles, we have been touched in some way by someone we love dealing with Substance Abuse Disorder. Many of us are unprepared to know what next steps we should take to guide us to thrive. If I told you there are, in fact, gifts and lessons to be discovered in the countless difficult moments you have faced with your addicted loved one, are facing, and will surely face in the future, would you believe me?

Voices InCourage is created to help guide families and loved ones to embrace a satisfying, healthy life with an addicted loved one in it, during crises and beyond them. It offers a new story about living with and loving those dealing with substance abuse disorder. This story is filled with resiliency, safety, joy, and vitality. This story reveals a growing community that is fully seen and heard with compassion and without judgment, a story of life beyond the wear-and-tear of crises, where thriving and living one's best life with an addicted loved one is entirely possible. This courageous community invites us to reawaken to a deeper love for ourselves and for those we love who are being crushed by this devastating disease.

Taking the First Step...

Do you know what you need in order to take your first healing step on this journey of discovery and transformation? I invite you to begin with this book. *The Five Acts of Courage: From Crisis to*

Thriving has been written with you in mind and is a reflection of my journey towards a life of healing, thriving, and hope. I wish this for you, too.

Your journey starts with The 5 Acts of Courage:

1 Allow for Feeling Emotions

2 Make Self-Care Non-Negotiable

3 Build a Powerful Community

4 Be Open to Changing Your Beliefs

5 Become an Active, Vigilant Learner

Out of devastation and heartbreak, I was determined to live my own best life, one that also embraced my grief as well as my pain and many unanswered questions. On my journey I discovered the inspiring resources and the kind of community I needed to *thrive*, not just simply survive one crisis after another. I began to seek the people, books, documentaries, videos, and podcasts whose messages illuminated my life's journey of possibility even in the midst of my son's disease. I chose to learn how to let go of wanting to fix Sam—wanting to relieve him of his suffering, really. Many moments of trial and error happened along my path to allow me to truly love him on his own journey. The questions I continue to ask myself are, "How do I navigate this crisis in a healthy, thriving way for myself?" "How do I love Sam unconditionally on this journey that he's on, as painful as it is to watch him suffer like this?"

Are you ready? Here we go.

KL Wells

Founder of Voices InCourage and mom of an addict

The 5
Acts of Courage

From Crisis to Thriving

When we're in crisis, especially prolonged crisis, we wonder whether we can survive it. We struggle and somehow we do survive this latest crisis, but often this is where our work ends—in relief that we have survived. Yet in survival mode we're still living fearfully. We're not confident, we're still nervous and sad. We may have trouble eating and sleeping, our moods may fluctuate, and we're unsure of who we are. We can be overwhelmed and irritable. We believe that if we can only effect a better outcome with our addicted loved one, we can relax and get back to our life again. We want to control what cannot be controlled. We're living at survival levels.

The following graphic (text supplied by the National Fallen Fighters Foundation), became an extraordinarily powerful tool for me to get clear about my own experience, create an intention, and set my course to move from crisis to thriving.

I believe that we have a choice to stay in crisis, struggling, just surviving or develop our skills, learn new ones, so that we'll be able to say to ourselves at some point, "I got this."

The Roadmap

in crisis	Struggling	surviving	Thriving
"I can't survive this."	"I can't keep this up."	"Something isn't right."	"I got this."

Disabling distress and loss of function

Panic attacks

Nightmares or flashbacks

Unable to fall or stay asleep

Intrusive thoughts

Thought of self-harm or suicide

Easily enraged or aggressive

Careless mistakes and inability to focus

Feeling numb, lost, or out of control

Withdraw from relationships

Dependence on substances, food, or other numbing activities to cope

Persistent fear, panic, anxiety, anger, pervasive sadness, hopelessness

Exhaustion

Poor performance and difficulty making decisions or concentrating

Avoiding interaction with coworkers, family, and friends

Fatigue, aches and pains

Restless, disturbed sleep

Self-medicating with substances, food or other numbing activities

Nervousness, sadness, increased mood fluctuations

Inconsistent performance

More easily overwhelmed or irritated

Increased need for control and difficulty adjusting to changes

Trouble sleeping or eating

Activities and relationships you used to enjoy seem less interesting or even stressful

Muscle tension, low energy, headaches

Calm and steady with minor mood fluctuations

Able to take things in stride

Consistent performance

Able to take feedback and to adjust to change of plans

Able to focus

Able to communicate effectively

Normal sleep patterns and appetite

1

Allow for feeling emotions

ALLOW FOR HUMANNESS

1
Allow for Feeling Emotions

After you've experienced a traumatic event, do you ever notice how many people ask you, "Are you OK?" How often have you automatically answered, "I'm fine," when it's clear to you and everyone else that you're not? How often have you swallowed your feelings and put on a brave face to stay in control? How often do we distract ourselves with activities like watching TV or scrolling the Internet or eating or drinking to excess, just to give ourselves some space from the tsunami of emotions churning below the surface?

What I know to be true is this: Life is messy. Stuff happens that causes us to feel. Healthy humans feel.

Yet we live in a culture that is very judgmental and ill-equipped to handle the emotions of being a human. Some believe displays of emotion are a sign of weakness, some don't want to deal with the messiness and, quite frankly, don't know how.

Even in that moment of watching Sam get arrested, I held my emotions just at the edge until I could get back in the hotel room. Once inside, I let it fly—all the grief, all the pain, all the panic tore through me. I was absolutely inconsolable.

That first brave step of feeling my emotions took an act of courage. Many times over the course of this journey I have cried and sobbed. I'm going to hold the space for you to do the same.

You may think that once you start crying, you might not be able to stop, so trust me when I say that you will stop. You will be exhausted when you do, and you will stop. I did.

Are you ready?

Allow for Feeling Emotions

Culturally, we're generally taught to repress our emotions.

Boys are taught to "suck it up!" and not to cry.

Men are considered weak if they cry, but anger is acceptable.

Girls and women are considered "emotional," meaning incapable.

Numbing our emotions with excess alcohol, drugs, TV bingeing, working, shopping, gambling, and eating has become socially acceptable.

Repressed emotions get stuck in our bodies and stifled feelings literally make us sick. Anger resides in the liver, grief prefers the lungs.

Blocked feelings are the barriers to joy, functional behavior, opening our hearts and later, even our physical health.

Which do you choose?

Negative energy is going to show up, but you can SHIFT YOUR RESPONSE so that you are the best version of yourself today!

NEGATIVE ENERGY   POSITIVE ENERGY

Allow for Feeling Emotions

Brain Science and Stress

Trauma, chaos, anger, fear—these all drive us to our brainstem, the place where we're caught in reaction mode. Making choices and decisions when we're in reaction and under great stress is never wise.

If possible, please take the time to shift from reaction and stress to calm and compassion. These are emotions that are available to you from the top of your mind, your neocortex.

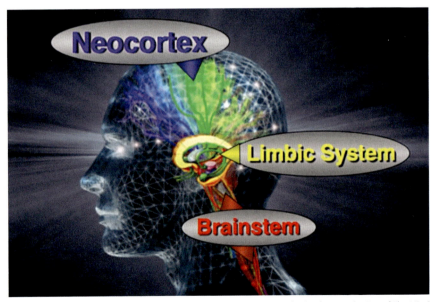

Image Source: Dr. Bill Crawford, *Life From the Top of The Mind*

Creativity, confidence, problem-solving and clarity all reside in our neocortex.

You want to reside in the neocortex!

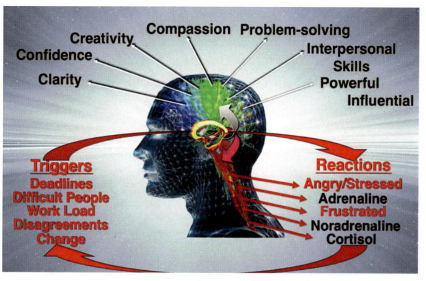

Image Source: Dr. Bill Crawford, *Life From the Top of The Mind*

The breathing tool on the next page is a simple and effective skill to help you shift to the top of your mind quickly.

Allow for Feeling Emotions

Counting is critical to be able to move from the brainstem to the neocortext of the brain. Because our brainstem can't count, this breathing practice is a powerful tool to shift out of survival reactions and responses.

TOOL: 4X4X4

Practice this breathing exercise to move from your brainstem to your neocortex.

Breathe in through your nose for 4 counts.

Hold your breath for 4 counts

Exhale for 4 counts.

4...4...4

TOOL: 3 KEYS TO EMOTIONAL TRANSFORMATION

Here are three keys to unlock powerful ways we can shift out of emotions that don't serve us.

1. Body

Each emotion has a physicality to it, which means you can shift your emotions by changing your body. The first step is awareness! When you recognize you feel negative emotions (anger, anxiety, sadness), then you are at choice. You can either remain in those emotions (which severely impact your ability to make decisions that serve your desired outcome) or you can choose to shift your emotions and create clarity, compassion and calm by changing your body.

For example, anger and sadness can be reflected in a contracted body posture. You can shift your emotional state by straightening up and extending your arms wide. You can also change your facial expression, like intentionally smiling (into a mirror, if possible) and shift your state of mind.

2. Focus

What you focus on, you get more of. This is a powerful thing to know. Again, your awareness gives you the opportunity to make a different choice—a choice that might help you navigate your experience at a more powerful level. For example, if I find myself constantly thinking that my son might die, it's never helpful. At night, it's easy for these thoughts to rise up. So I choose to shift to meditative breathing first and then focus on three things that I'm most grateful for.

3. Language

Pay attention to the negative thoughts and words you're using. Interrupting them by declaring gratitude OUT LOUD (for something not even related to your distress) can shift your energy and give you a fresh perspective. There is power in using your voice!

I RECOGNIZE THAT

nothing is personal.

—*The Four Agreements* by Don Miguel Ruiz

2

Make self-care non-negotiable

PUT YOUR OXYGEN MASK ON FIRST

2

Make Self-Care Non-Negotiable

I've had a very robust regimen of self care most of my professional life, and yet, when I learned about Sam's drug addiction and life-threatening risks, especially with his use of fentanyl, I knew I had to elevate my level of self-care quickly. The stakes were higher and out of necessity I was compelled to prioritize my self-care at a higher level that I *did not negotiate away.*

As Sam's risks increased, I optimized my self-care and began learning about maximizing the quality of my sleep. I refined my food choices and eating habits, increased my exercise program, and deepened my spiritual practices. I also paid attention to what brought me joy—petting my cat, uplifting music, massages, enjoying one of Patty's great meals. I made sure I touched joy on a daily basis.

Putting ourselves at the top of our list of people we take care of is probably one of the most important acts of courage we can do.

Are you ready?

Make Self-Care Non-Negotiable

COMMIT TO A DAILY EMOTION & ENERGY MANAGEMENT PLAN

Importance of morning routines

Morning routines are foundational to your day.

Be intentional — Create YOUR plan for the day.

Exercise — Make time to move 4-5 times per week.

This can be weight training, cardio, going to the gym, walking, yoga, etc.

3 Keystone Habits

1. Great Sleep
2. Meditation
3. 30 Minutes of Walking

COMMIT TO A DAILY EMOTION & ENERGY MANAGEMENT PLAN

Know how & when to shift your environment

Spend time out in nature daily (walking, gardening, hiking, kayaking, backpacking).

Enjoy inspirational music, dancing, reading, videos.

Disconnect from the news & your cell phone regularly!

Super Important:

Ask for Help!

If you need something, learn to ask!

Make Self-Care Non-Negotiable

HAPPINESS CHEMICALS & HOW TO HACK THEM

DOPAMINE The Chemical Reward	OXYTOCIN The Love Hormone
• Completing a task • Doing self-care activities • Eating food • Celebrating little wins	• Playing with a dog • Playing with a baby • Holding a hand • Hugging your family • Giving a compliment

HAPPINESS CHEMICALS & HOW TO HACK THEM

SEROTONIN The Mood Stabilizer	ENDORPHIN The Pain Killer
• Meditating • Running • Sun exposure • Walk in nature • Swimming • Cycling	• Laughter • Essential oils • Watch a comedy • Dark chocolate • Exercising

3

Build a powerful community

**INSPIRATIONAL PEOPLE
& COMMUNITY**

3

Build a Powerful Community

I can't overemphasize this enough: ***The #1 factor that will determine whether you're going to thrive in the midst of managing crises around this disease—or not—is the quality of people you interact with every day.*** According to John Maxwell, 95% of our success or failure in life is directly determined by the 6-8 people with whom we routinely surround ourselves.

Having people to turn to in a crisis has immense power, but be aware that who you turn to has the power to either bring you up or take you down. Are they life-giving or life-sucking? I chose life-giving, of course, and so was very intentional about surrounding myself with people who loved Sam and me without judgment. I built a spiritual community and embarked on a nine-month Vision Quest process. Beyond a shadow of a doubt, this community supported me and loved me in the midst of one of the most intense periods of my life.

In addition, I created a business master-mind group that held a safe place for me to express myself personally and professionally. I shared the good, the bad, and the ugly with them. They have cried with me and held me, laughed with me, and became extraordinarily powerful in holding me in this space of healing and wellness.

How powerful is your own community? Perhaps it's time to make some changes.

Are you ready?

Build a Powerful Community

THE POWER OF COMMUNITY

95% of your success is directly determined by who you surround yourself with on a regular basis.

Who you surround yourself with is who you become!

A positive community will:

- Lift you up

- Have your back

- Never take sides

- Inspire you to be the next best version of yourself

Ask yourself:

Are your friends or relationships aligned with an outcome versus the journey?

Are they in the right position to help you through this process?

Example:

Some people are very judgmental about the choices (for instance, lying) your loved one may make during their addiction.

I personally prefer to surround myself with a community that recognizes that lying is part of the disease and I never get caught up in "fact-checking." No matter what behaviors my loved one displays dealing with this disease, I'm in this for the long haul... the journey.

And, I'm clear that I have no idea when my loved one will get help.

Building Community

TOOL: LAUGHING BUDDY

Laughter is a powerful experience to shift our energy.

When you are not feeling good or need a pick-me-up, call the person who makes you laugh the most!

4

Be open to changing your beliefs

**WE RISE TO THE LEVEL OF THE
QUESTIONS WE ASK OURSELVES**

4

Be Open to Changing Your Beliefs

One of the most dynamic tools that will determine the quality of your journey from crisis to thriving is your willingness to examine your belief systems and pay attention to the questions you ask yourself—you know, those questions that keep rolling around in your head in the middle of the night.

What I've grown to accept along my journey over decades of generational trauma is that questioning the unquestioned beliefs we have is paramount to thriving from trauma.

For instance, when I learned that Sam was using fentanyl, the first thing I asked myself was, "What are the gifts and lessons embedded in this?" I know this sounds crazy, and yet I knew there was something I didn't know that I needed to know. I went to my bookshelves and grabbed two books. The first was *Loving What Is: Four Questions That Can Change Your Life* by Byron Katie and second was *A New Earth: Awakening to Your Life's Purpose* by Eckhart Tolle. Those books gave me more of a sense of peace that, honestly, I still can't quite explain. What I do know about myself is that when I come up against the edge of pain that is so debilitating, it causes me to want to investigate it and adopt different perspectives and beliefs. I've done this throughout my life. Challenging my own beliefs, especially in a crisis, has become a rewarding process of exploration that continues to evolve.

What beliefs do you hold today that are keeping you from thriving in the midst of chaos?

Are you ready?

Be Open to Changing Your Beliefs

MINDSET IS A SKILL SET THAT CAN BE LEARNED!

Are you asking empowering questions or asking disempowering questions?

What we inherently believe plays itself out in our behaviors and actions.

You need to make sure that your beliefs are serving the best version of you.

You're in the flow of change: Who you are today is not who you will be tomorrow, a year or five years from now.

You'll learn from these new tools and you'll acquire the skills that will help you become more of the person you want to be.

WHAT ARE THE QUESTIONS YOU ASK YOURSELF?

No matter how intense my challenges are, the question that I lean into all the time is:

WHAT ARE THE

gifts and lessons

EMBEDDED IN THIS EXPERIENCE?

Be Open to Changing Your Beliefs

This one question has shifted everything for me.

Step into the question.

Search for the answers.

There will be gifts and lessons that will move you forward!

LIFE DOESN'T HAPPEN TO US — IT HAPPENS FOR US!

THIS IS **NOT** MY RESPONSIBILITY

Other people's words

Other people's ideas

Other people's mistakes

THIS **IS** MY RESPONSIBILITY

My words, my behavior, my actions, my efforts, my mistakes, my ideas & the consequences of my actions

Other people's opinions

Other people's beliefs

Other people's actions

The consequences of other people's actions

5

Become an active, vigilant learner

BE CURIOUS

5

Become an Active, Vigilant Learner

I use the word "vigilant" here—alert and on the lookout for opportunity—because that's what it's taken for me to continue to learn. I've been an active, vigilant learner since my early teens, seeking people with wisdom and knowledge about what I want to learn and know, listening, reading books, finding ways I can elevate how to think about what matters to me and what doesn't, learning how I process information and events, what my beliefs and perspectives are, and so on. The learning never stops; I have embraced an intensive course of personal development that continues to expand and strengthen me throughout my lifetime.

The crisis with Sam and his journey cracked me so wide open that I became compelled to learn something new every day. His disease urged me to get a "Ph.D", so to speak, in being human. Sam's journey caused me to become more focused in my own learning and self-expansion than I could have ever thought possible, and for that I am so grateful.

As you travel your own journey, I wish this active exploration and vigilant learning for you, too.

Are you ready?

Become an Active, Vigilant Learner

We are so blessed to learn from the knowledge and experiences of others. They are available to us right now!

- Podcasts

- Online Trainings

- YouTube Videos

- Books

- Coaches

GREAT PEOPLE
GREAT LEADERS
GREAT BOOKS

All these resources can help us expand our perspectives and shift us from who we are in this moment to who we want to be in the next.

Become a great student of whoever it is you want to be.

TOOL: FINDING SUCCESSFUL ROLE MODELS IS ONE OF THE MOST POWERFUL WAYS TO LEARN AND CHANGE.

Learn from other people who have arrived at the place you are heading towards.

success leaves clues

—Jim Rohn

You are not alone in this journey.

We are all on this journey.

We are all in various places in this journey.

There are people who can help.

Do you know someone who has navigated through this experience successfully and can be a resource?

Become an Active, Vigilant Learner

DISCOVER: IF YOU DON'T KNOW ALREADY, FIND YOUR PREDOMINANT LEARNING STYLE.

Example:

Our school system is geared for auditory learners. Not every learning system will apply to you. Are you:

Visual? You might learn best when seeing pictures, videos, webinars, movies, books ...

Kinesthetic? Your best learning experience is when you're moving or doing. For example, lots of people in the trades learn best by doing the trade.

Auditory? Podcasts are great examples of auditory learning. If you're someone who hears it and remembers it easily, you're auditory.

Do you prefer podcasts, videos, online training, books, in-person training or private coaching? When you've wanted to learn something new that was super important to you, what was your best way to learn it?

Pick **ONE** of the tools that inspires and helps you the most and work with that tool consistently. It will change your life.

Create habits that serve

CONSCIOUS **CHOICES**

BETTER **HABITS**

FOCUSED **INTENTIONS**

NEW **SKILL SETS**

As we learn how to navigate our personal journeys in healthy, conscious and intentional ways, we own our own decisions and we thrive.

We then become a teacher, a role model and a guide.

We are all here to serve, in some form or fashion.

To each one of you reading this: **You Are That Person!**

Begin now!

Who do you **CHOOSE** to be?

It is yours to **DECIDE**.

With your wise choices, you can **THRIVE**
and have your best life!

We Invite You To Join Our Community.

Sign Up at Voicesincourage.com

About the Author

KL Wells

• • •

Executive coach, author, community leader, influential speaker, and mother, KL Wells provides inspiring state-of-the-art training and impactful consulting to CEOs and business owners. She advises her clients on business strategies, strategic networking, and revenue generation to foster effective and influential business leaders in successful companies.

More recently KL's mission to help families and parents of addicted loved ones has inspired her to launch Voices InCourage. This emerging community provides important resources to courageous individuals who seek to heal, connect, and thrive as they face some of the most challenging times in their lives.

KL was raised both in the Washington, D.C., area and on a 20,000-acre Montana cattle ranch just north of Yellowstone National Park. The daughter of an Episcopalian minister, she grew up surrounded by three generations of successful entrepreneurs...and cowboys.

Resources

Voices InCourage

Book Recommendations

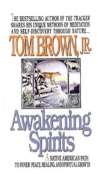

**Awakening Spirits:
A Native American Path
to Inner Peace, Healing
and Spiritual Growth**

by Tom Brown, Jr.

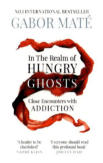

*In the Realm
of Hungry Ghosts*

by Dr. Gabor Mate

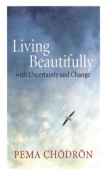

*Living Beautifully
with Uncertainty
and Change*

by Pema Chodron

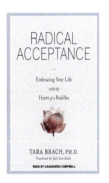

**Radical Acceptance:
Embracing Your Life
with the Heart of a Buddha**

by Tara Brach, Ph.D.

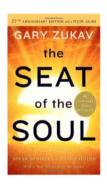

Seat of the Soul

by Gary Zukav

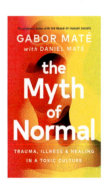

**The Myth of Normal:
Trauma, Illness & Healing
in a Toxic Culture**

by Dr. Gabor Mate

Resources

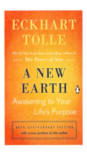

A New Earth: Awakening to Your Life's Purpose
by Eckhart Tolle

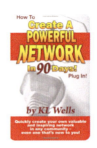

How to Create a Powerful Network in 90 Days
by KL Wells

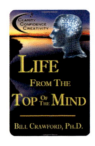

Life from The Top of the Mind
by Bill Crawford, PhD

Loving What Is: Four Questions That Can Change Your Life
by Byron Katie

The Happiness Advantage
by Shawn Achor

Rising Strong
by Brene Brown

Anatomy of the Spirit: The Seven Stages of Power and Healing
by Caroline Myss

Unstoppable: 45 Powerful Stories of Perseverance and Triumph from People Just Like You
by Cynthia Kersey

You Can Heal Your Life
by Louise Hay

Thrive: The Third Metric to Redefining Success and Creating a Life of Well-Being, Wisdom and Wonder
by Arianna Huffington

Jesus Calling: Peace in His Presence
by Sarah Young

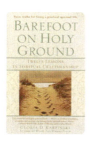

Barefoot on Holy Ground: Twelve Lessons in Spiritual Craftsmanship
by Gloria Karpinski

The Body Keeps the Score: Brain, Mind and Body in the Healing of Trauma
by Bessel Van Der Kolk, M.D

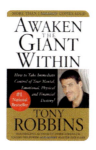

Awaken the Giant Within
by Anthony Robbins

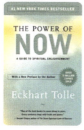

The Power of NOW: A Guide to Spiritual Enlightenment
by Eckhart Tolle

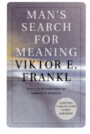

Man's Search for Meaning
by Victor Frankl

The Four Agreements
by Don Miguel Ruiz

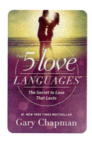

The Five Love Languages: The Secret to Love that Lasts
by Gary Chapman

Resources

[The Paradigm Conspiracy](#)
by Christopher Largent &
Denise Breton

[When Things Fall Apart: Heart
Advice for Difficult Times](#)
by Pema Chodron

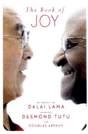

[The Book of Joy: Lasting
Happiness in a Changing World](#)
by The Dalai Lama & Desmond
Tutu

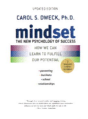

[Mindset: The New Psychology
of Success](#)
by Carol Dweck, Ph.D.

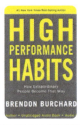

[High Performance Habits: How
Extraordinary People Become
That Way](#)
by Brendon Burchard

[Emotional Intelligence 2.0](#)
by Travis Bradberry & Jean
Greaves

[You Are a Badass: How to Stop
Doubting Your Greatness and
Start Living an Awesome Life
Part of: You Are a Badass® (3
Books)](#)
By Jen Sincero

Specific to Voices InCourage

American Fix: Inside the Opioid Addiction Crisis and How to End It
by Ryan Hampton

Codependency No More and The New Codependency
by Melody Beattie

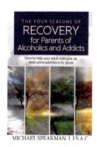

The Four Seasons of RECOVERY for Parents of Alcoholics and Addicts: How to Help Your Child Give Up Destructive Addictions for Good
by Michael Speakman, L.I.S.A.C.

Under Our Roof: A Son's Battle for Recovery, a Mother's Battle for Her Son
by Madeleine Dean & Harry Cunnane

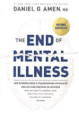

The End of Mental Illness
by Daniel Amen, MD

Resources

Specific to Voices InCourage

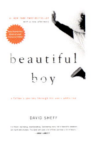

Beautiful Boy
by David Sheff

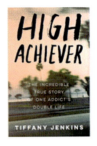

High Achiever: The Incredible True Story of One Addict's Double Life
by Tiffany Jenkins

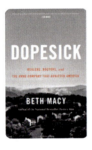

Dopesick: Dealers, Doctors, and The Drug Company That Addicted America
by Beth Macy

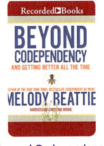

Beyond Codependency
 by Melody Beattie

Powerful Video

Pleasure Unwoven: a personal journey about addiction
by Kevin McCauley

Made in the USA
Middletown, DE
06 March 2024

50827226R00033